A Snapshot Of Denton

A Journey in Pictures around the Village

Compiled by

THE INHABITANTS

ERSKINE PRESS

2000

Published in 2000 by The Erskine Press
Twin Cottage, Middle Road, Denton, Norfolk

ISBN 1 85297 065 0

British Library Cataloguing-in-Publication Data
A catalogue record for this book is
available from the British Library

Typeset by Waveney Typesetters, Wymondham, Norfolk
Printed in Great Britain by Barnwell's of Aylsham, Aylsham, Norfolk

Title page illustration: A view across Denton Fields   *Guyton*

Thank You

This book could not have been produced without the hard work, enthusiasm and commitment of the people of Denton.

We had to complete the project, from start to finish, in nine months – in March, this seemed a formidable task. Nevertheless, the enthusiastic way in which everybody took to the project made light of it, and to all of you who took time to contribute a big 'thank you' for making this possible.

However, a few people deserve special thanks:

- Barbara Spaul for drawing the maps of the five routes around the village,
- Moss Chemist in Harleston for arranging the processing and printing of the photographs and providing us with a discount,
- the editorial team – Adele Godsmark, Anne Carden, Steve Whiteman, Terry and Kath Hanner – for wading tirelessly through more than 3,000 photographs
- and Stephen Easton for his professional advice, unfailing zeal and technical expertise.

Finally, we are extremely grateful to The National Lottery Millennium Festival Awards For All who provided the grant enabling us to produce our own photographic account of rural life in Norfolk in the summer of the year 2000.

Annie Whiteman

Official Supporter

Made possible by the National Lottery

Why this book?

As part of our millennium celebrations in the village we agreed that it was important to have some lasting record of life in our village at the turn of the millennium. Two projects were agreed upon. A ledger, recording information about those living in the village and a book attempting to capture life in Denton, in photographs taken by those who live here.

The ledger has been written by residents in the village and compiled by Jenny Crohill (with the help of Sandy Jones) from the village and provides a fascinating insight into people's lives and histories.

In contrast we agreed that this book – **A Snapshot of Denton** – should be just that, **a snapshot**. In time we hope that some enterprising souls with time on their hands will write a history of our village. This book is a record of how the people of Denton see their village in the year 2000 and does not attempt to capture its history. What we hope is that in 50 or 100 year's time, people will be fascinated by these photographs of daily life in Denton just as we were by the hundreds of old photographs put together in an exhibition this year by Terry and Kathryn Hanner as part of our millennium celebrations.

How the book was compiled

Having been lucky enough to receive a grant from the National Lottery, we were able to offer every household in Denton a free film and processing or a free instant camera. We wanted as many people as possible to take part and so all households received individual invitations to join in with the project. Of the 157 households in the village 128 contributed to the book – a remarkable achievement!

Rik Martin with Annie Whiteman

In late May we held a book 'launch' where Rik Martin, a photography lecturer, gave us some hints on what makes a good photograph and films were handed out along with hamburgers and hotdogs.

The final book has been put together by a team of editors who have attempted to reflect Denton as it is today. Surrounded by thousands of photographs it has taken many hours to narrow down the possible entries to this final version. We have tried hard to avoid over-emphasising the more 'picturesque' parts of Denton and those buildings which have more history. The book has been divided into five geographical sections and a

The editing team at work

final section covers our millennium celebrations. As its title suggests, we have aimed to produce *a snapshot* of our village captured by its inhabitants in the summer of the year 2000. Everyone who took part in the project should find themselves represented.

Denton – the village

The parish of Denton lies in rural South Norfolk with the river Waveney forming its southern boundary. To the east lie Earsham and Bungay. Bedingham and Topcroft lie to the north and Alburgh is to the south and west. Hardwick borders the far boundary to the north-west. At the last census in 1991 the population stood at 360. Many of the inhabitants are newcomers to the village but there are some residents with long connections. These include: The Pointers, The Fairheads, The Skinners, The Sheldrakes, The Talbots, The Nobbs, The Battells, The Hanners, The Guntons, The Townsends, The Winters, The Walkers and The Thomas family.

Denton is a friendly and sociable village where those people who want to join in are welcomed and encouraged. Since the closure of the village shop in 1991 the village hall has become the centre of much of village activity. This currently includes Indoor Bowls, Friendly Club, Denton Variety Club, Women's Institute, Gardening Club and Lawn Tennis Club. On Friday evenings the bar is open and is an important meeting place for many people.

As well as holding services our church and chapel provide venues for other activities. One morning a week there is a post office at the Chapel and coffee is served by volunteers who encourage people to stay and catch up on news and gossip! The church is used occasionally for concerts including the one that formed part of our millennium celebrations.

Much of the village is surrounded by agricultural land. Changes in farming practice mean that there is currently only one farm in the village that still has a herd of dairy cows. This is at Low Farm near the southern border of Denton. When landowners were given the opportunity to take land out of cultivation in the 1980s one of our major landowners took up the opportunity. The village gained about 800 acres of land that could be used temporarily for dog-walking, horse-riding or simply by people wanting to enjoy the wildlife which has established itself. This wildlife includes skylarks and bee orchids.

Most children in the village travel to Alburgh with Denton Nursery and First School to begin their education. (Denton School closed down in the late 1970s). They then transfer to Canon Pickering Junior School and Archbishop Sancroft High School in Harleston, although some move on to schools in Bungay or elsewhere. For those who stay on to study at 'A' level most travel to Diss High School, Bungay High School or to the Hewett School or City College in Norwich.

Many adults travel some distance to work and most households rely on at least one car. We have a very limited public transport system and a Community Bus run by volunteers which provide a vital service for villagers without their own transport.

In February Denton was the first village in Norfolk to plant a Millennium Wood. Over 200 people turned out to plant trees and to be part of history. We hope that in years to come people may enjoy glancing through this book as they sit in the shade of a magnificent oak tree in the Millennium Wood.

Links with Denton, Texas, USA

When the planning for the Millennium Wood began in early 1999 the group involved thought it would be a good idea to contact a Denton in another country to see if they might give financial support. They carried out an internet search finding two Dentons in the USA with internet addresses and websites and sent them messages containing the plans for the wood and asking for support.

Lorraine Macgregor from the Parks Department in Denton, Texas was very interested. They already had in progress a 'Legacy Wood' in their South Lakes Park where they were planting indigenous trees with people's sponsorship. Despite a big difference in population (theirs is 75,000 and growing whilst ours is a steady 350 or so) they decided after lots of e-mails to set up an informal twinning arrangement with them.

One Sunday in November 1999 The Squirrell Family had a surprise e-mail from Euline and Horace Brock of Denton, Texas. They were on business in London and hoped to visit Denton, Norfolk. They visited on the Tuesday after some hasty arrangements were made and enjoyed a good day in Denton. They enjoyed a traditional lunch and planted two American Red Oak Trees in our wood. Euline Brock is very interested in preserving the environment and was enthusiastic about our project. She has since been elected Mayor of Denton Texas. Both Communities agreed to plant trees in their woods and dedicate them to the other Denton.

On February 6th 2000 while we were planting and officially opening our wood, a grove of trees was dedicated to us in a ceremony on South Lakes Park with a memorial which reads;

> 'This grove is dedicated to the villagers of Denton, Norfolk, England.
> In Friendship. By the Denton Park Foundation.'

We have similarly honoured them in our wood.

Denton Texas so liked our idea of marking the millennium by planting a wood that they decided to create their own Millennium Wood with people sponsoring trees. Their wood was dedicated on September 23rd 2000. Euline Brock gave the opening speech to which we contributed a message of goodwill and friendship hoping that the relationship between our two communities can flourish and grow as our Millennium Woods grow in the future.

A brief history of Denton

The word Denton is believed to mean 'home in a hollow'. Given the original location of the village down by the church, this would make sense. It is believed to date from Saxon times. At the northern extreme of the village along Darrow Green Road there are the remains of an old motte and bailey castle believed to have been built by William d'Albini who then went on to build the rather grander castle at New Buckenham. This may have been his hunting lodge. The name Darrow Green probably derives from 'deerhaugh' meaning 'deer park' and wild deer can still occasionally be spotted on the road. (The site of the castle was bought by the National Trust a few years ago.)

St Mary's Church at the southern end of the village dates from the 12th Century and is very large for such a small parish. It has a magnificent stained glass east window. In the fourteenth century many peasants lived in cottages in the valley to the west of the church. When the Black Death struck many village people died and their houses may have been burned down as part of the cleansing of the area. 'New' houses were built further up the village away from the area of disease. Several of these timber-framed houses are still standing today – although some hide their origins behind much more modern frontages.

The well-known writer Rider Haggard, writing at the turn of the century has a strong connection with Denton. He owned Haggards Farm on Chapel Hill (currently owned by the Fairhead family) which is mentioned in his famous book 'A Farming Year'. The Skinner family, still resident in Denton, are mentioned in the book as his tenants.

Denton United Reformed Chapel dates back to 1658. It was founded by a 'wandering preacher' from Wattisham who founded the original congregational chapel. The present building dates from 1821. All the surrounding chapels (Bungay and Harleston) were 'offspring' of the mother chapel in Denton.

At the opposite end of Darrow Green Road from Denton castle there was a wooden post mill active until the 1900s. Three nearby houses Mill House, Mill Farm (now Mutts Farm) and Mill Cottage (now Mill Farm) would probably have housed families associated with the mill.

During the second world war there were a number of American airfields including those at Topcroft and Hardwick right on the boundary of the village. The sudden effect of 2000 young American males being stationed less than a mile away as the crow flies had a huge impact. Some of them cycled to Denton on Wednesday evening to the village 'social'. Mrs Knights the schoolteacher thumped out waltzes and quicksteps on the piano at more or less the same tempo. One memorable night a USAF lorry arrived complete with American band and musical instruments. There was much laughter and jitterbugging but the local chaps were not so keen to see their village 'invaded'. There wasn't any actual fighting but choice words were exchanged between the Americans and the locals. By the next week it was back to Mrs Knights and her waltzes. By the end of the war some 80,000 British women became GI brides including three from the village of Denton.

Denton House at the southern end of the village was used as a convalescence home for servicemen during the war years.

Denton Village Hall was built in 1923. Prior to its building the Women's Institute met in the chapel vestry and whist drives were held at the school. During World War Two it was used as a school for evacuees. It remained very much as it was originally built until the 1990s when it was modernised and extended. A new bar and toilets transformed the place. It is now the hub of village life.

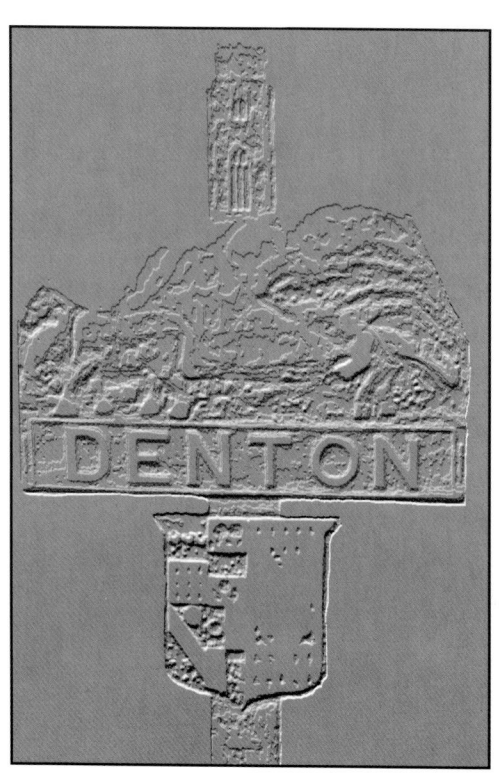

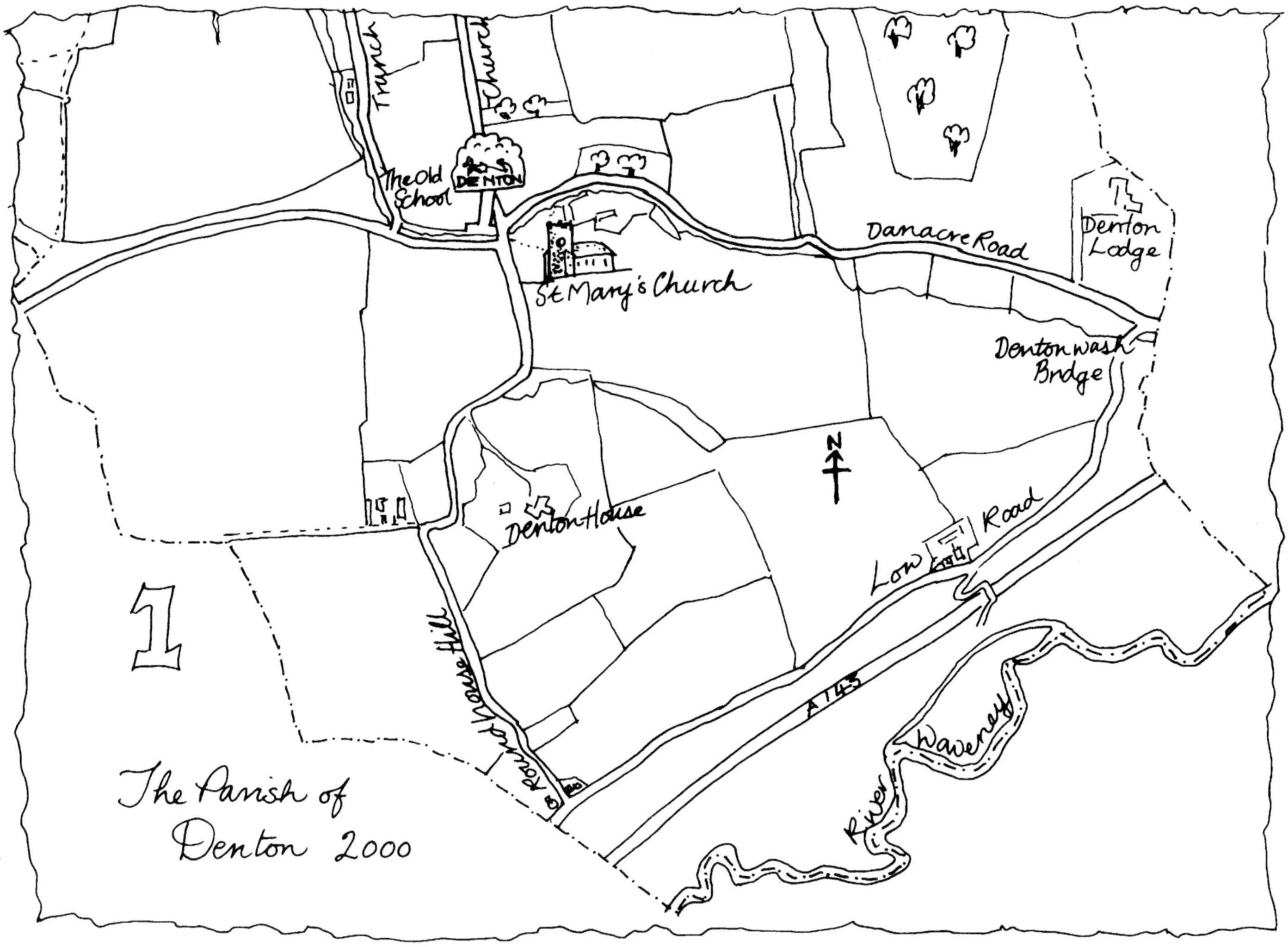
Trunch
Church
The Old School
DENTON
St Mary's Church
Danacre Road
Denton Lodge
Dentonwash Bridge
N
Denton House
Low Road
A143
River Waveney
Roundhouse Hill
1
The Parish of Denton 2000

ALBURGH 1
DENTON ¾
NORWICH 15
EARSHAM 2¾
3¾
HEDENHAM
WORTWELL 1¾
HARLESTON 4

Ashton

Helen Wallace

Wallace

Danacre Road

Hewlett

The lych gate   *Martin*

Eighteenth-century grave stones   *Jones*

The Church of St Mary the Virgin, Denton   *Ashton*

3

The isolated position of the Parish Church is probably due to its being built near one of the chief residences of the village in Saxon times. The Western Norman round tower has been strangely restored, part in brick and part in flint, after the original tower collapsed in the early 1500s.

The main feature inside is the huge East Window – a patchwork of stained glass collected by the Reverend Matthew Postlethwaite after the Restoration.

Thomas

Hill

Roy Day bringing the water supply to the Church

Whipps

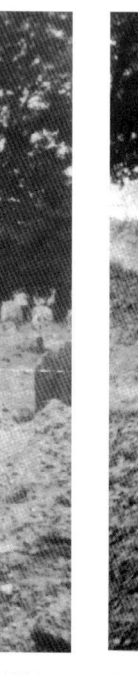

Gravestone

Ready

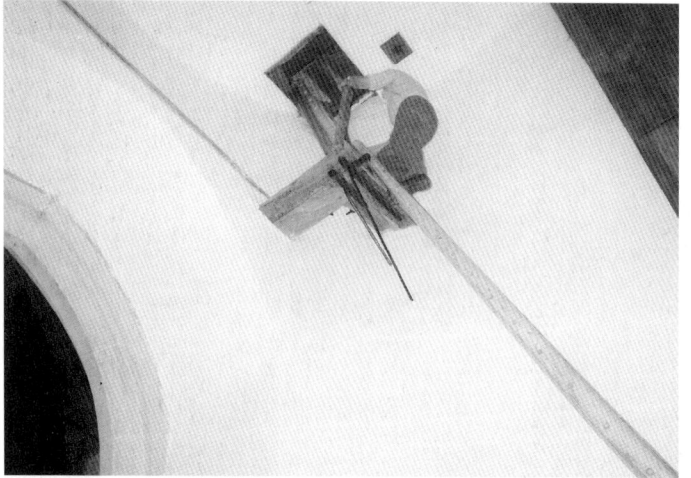

Thomas

Tim Thomas climbing the ladder and winding the church clock

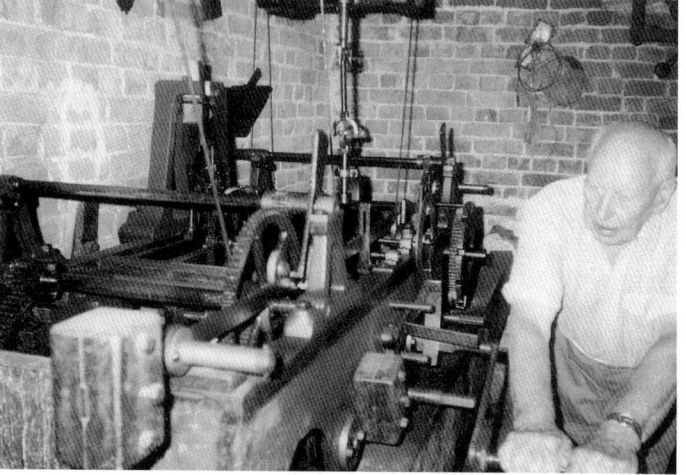

Thomas

4

The Old Rectory

de Bernières-Smart

Cathy Gill

de Bernières-Smart

Captain Corelli's mandolin

de Bernières-Smart

de Bernières-Smart

Rectory Cottage

Jones

Billy Jones with Thomas

de Bernières-Smart

Sandy Jones

Jones

6

Entrance to Denton Lodge

Darell

Trimming the yew hedge   *Darell*

Jeffrey Darell showing the size of the Great Oak   *Darell*

Bridget Darell   *Darell*

Denton Lodge   *Darell*

Marshes, Low Farm, June flood

Whipps

Andrew and Shirley Palmer, Rosie and Christopher

Palmer

Harvesting

Whipps

The Paddocks, Low Road

Balls

The Round House   *Mayhew*

Home Farm, Round House Hill   *Hewlett*

Off to the Ball, Brian Hewlett and Malcolm Reid   *Hewlett*

Home Farm   *Hewlett*

The interior of the grotto has seashells embedded in the walls. It is said that these shells were brought back from New Zealand on the return of Captain Cook's *Endeavour* in 1771. As Bert Weigman says 'It would be nice if it was true!'

The Parish Council Site Meeting to the Grotto, Denton House

Carden

The Folly

Weigman

Thomas and Benedict

Whipps

Bert and Gail Weigman and family outside Denton House

Weigman

10

Farm track by Home Farm

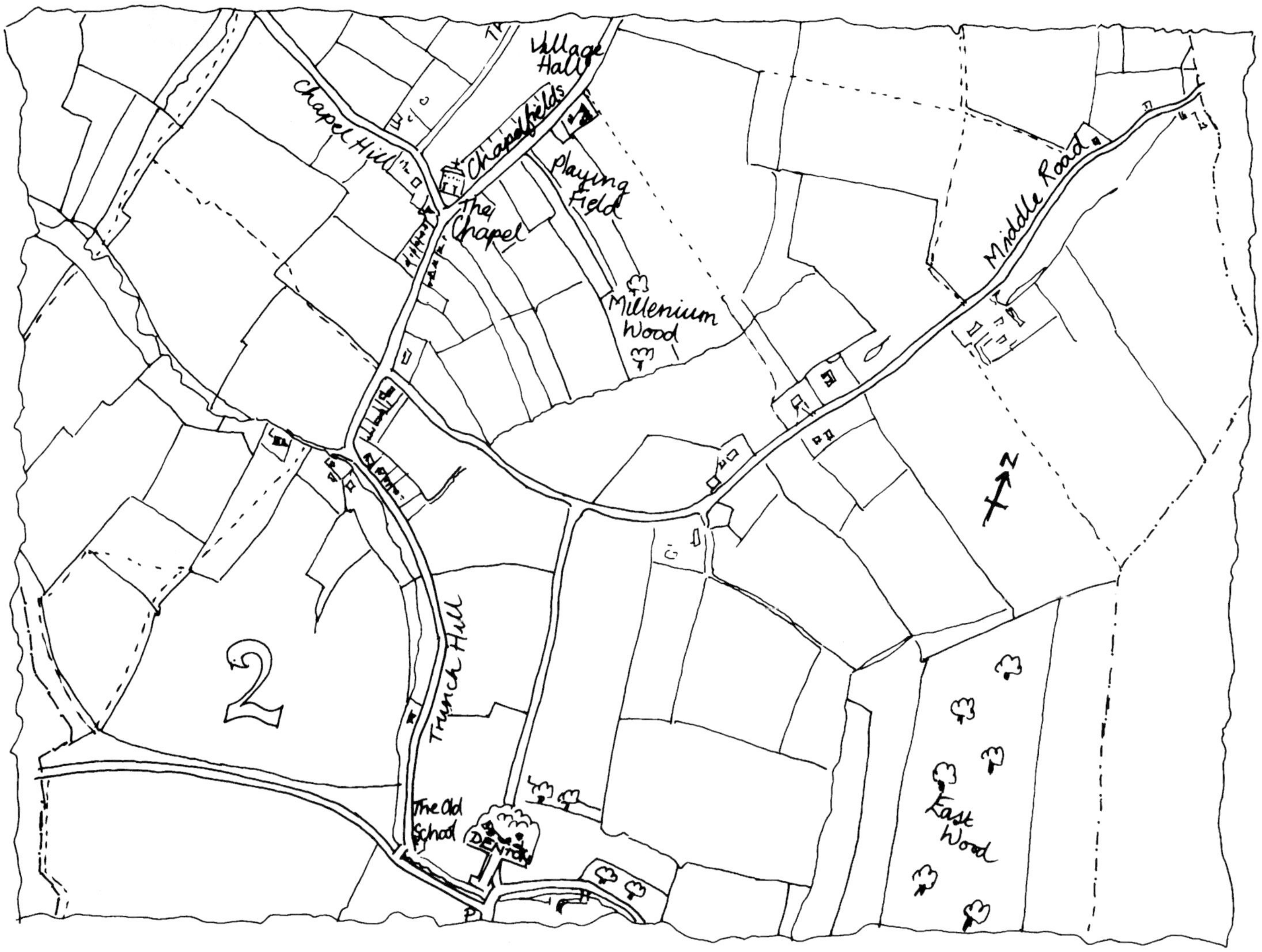

Liz Cargill cleaning up the village

D. Battell

The Old School House   *Fennessy*

Katrina, Siobahn and Davina Cattermole   *Cattermole*

Four West Highlands lead the way   *Cattermole*

The Old School   *Austen*

Flash flood, June 2000, Trunch Hill   *Clues*

Clues

Trunch House
Gregory

Trisha Gregory
Carden

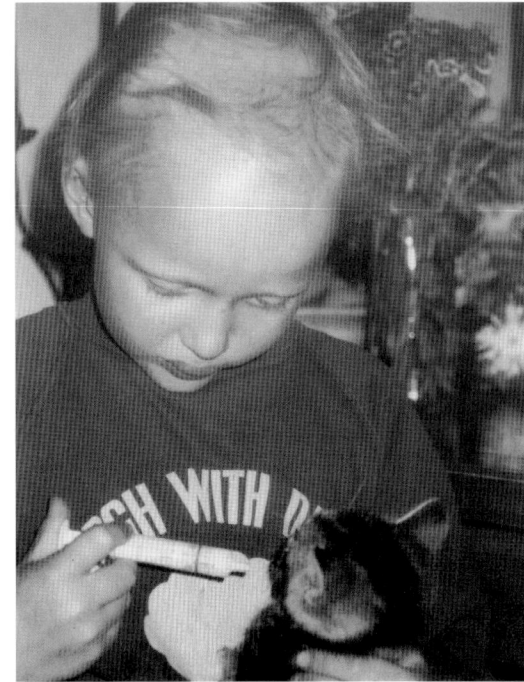

Fleur Guyton
Guyton

Hillside
Hooker

A part of the garden at Beck Farm

Charnick

The field above Vale Farm

Guyton

16

The Beck by Vale Farm   *Cable*

Vale Farm   *Charnick*

Vale Farm   Peel

Pearl and Tony Charnick   *Wallace*

Nigel Seamons at Beck Farm
Wallace

Trunch Hill   *Roper*

Summer Party, Trunch Hill
Reeder

Rachel Cable and Rae Stribling with Nicole
Stribling

Ernie Sheldrake
Reeder

Cable

Rachel and Stuart Cable
Reeder

Rebecca, Zoe, Alexandra, Rachel, Sadie and Joshua   *Cable*

The ice-cream van   *Cable*

Zoe and Sadie Stribling   *Stribling*

Luke, Gemma, Amie, Rebecca, Sadie, Zoe, Jade and Rachel   *Stribling*

Getting on the school bus   *Stribling*

Helen Everson   *Everson*

Rae Stribling and Amie   *Everson*

Jean Hanner   *M. Hanner*

Jade and Luke Shaw   *Shaw*

Dick and Stanley Sheldrake   *R. Sheldrake*

21

Sawyers

Ready

Pear Tree Cottage

Roper

E. Sheldrake

Ready

Kingsland Farm   *Valori*

Charlotte Valori   *Valori*

Katherine, Charlotte, Alex, Philip and Claire Valori   *Valori*

View towards Denton Millennium Wood

Gibson

Grove Cottage

Gibson

![Hall Farm photograph]

Hall Farm   *T. Barber*

This modern-looking house replaced Denton Hall, an extensive building.

Tim and Tom Barber   *T. Barber*

Mobile sawmill   *T. Barber*

Northside and Bramble Cottages   *Sutton*

Robert Sutton   *Sutton*

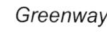

Cindy, Jules and Daniel Greenway   *Greenway*

Hall Farm Barns   *Greenway*

East Hall (previously Lodge Farm)   *Sprake*

David, Debbie, Charlie, Lydia and Richard Sprake   *Sprake*

Fiona Easton   *Easton*

Twin Cottage   *Easton*

27

George Pointer and Brenda Day

R. Day

George Pointer

Martin

Ronnie Sheldrake

Martin

George Pointer

R. Sheldrake

George Pointer

Martin

Boundary Farm

Gibson

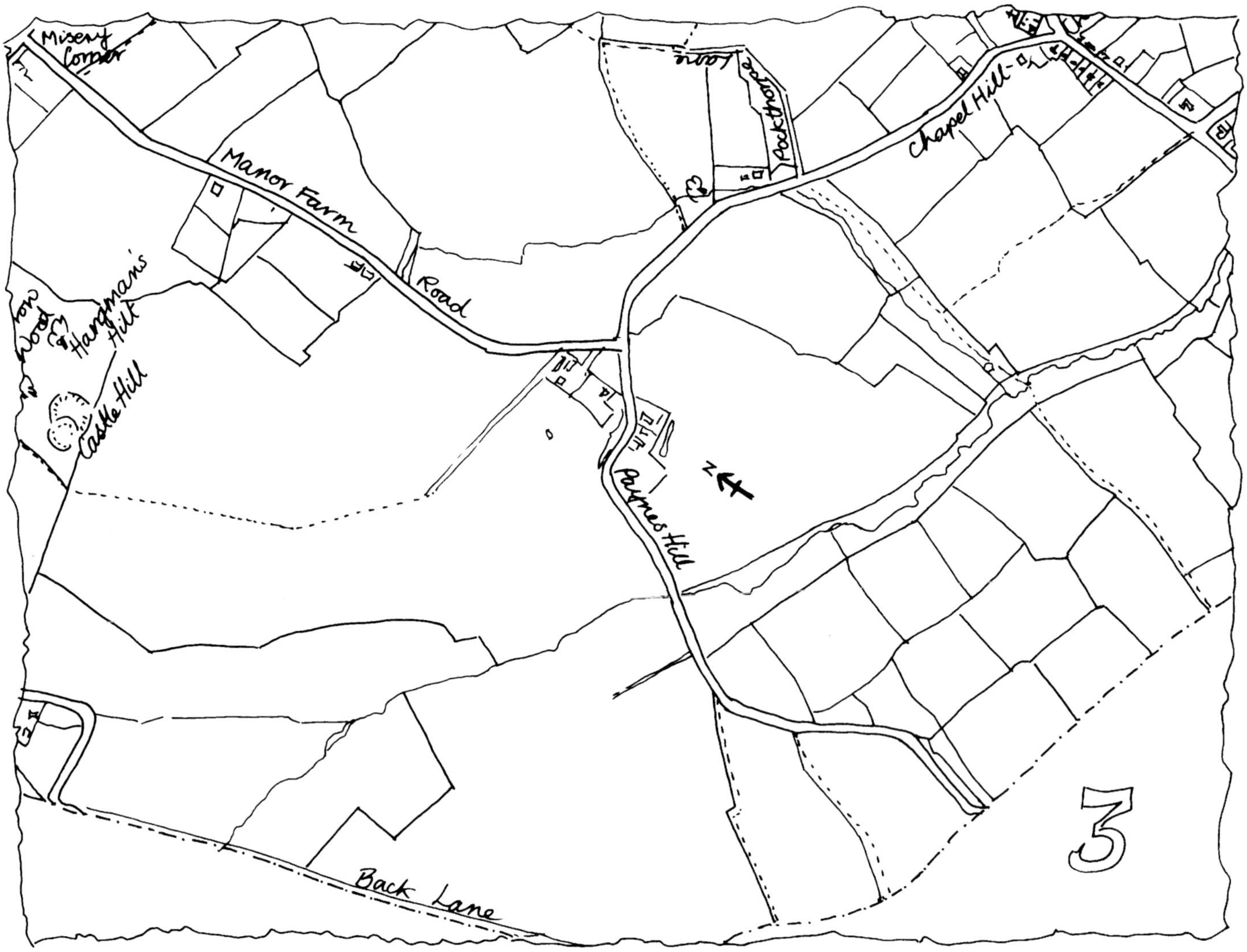

Jenny Crohill and Nigel Seamons

Crohill

The Watch House, a timber framed house was one of the two public houses in Denton until it closed in the early 1960s

G. Fairhead

Califer

A. Fairhead

Malvina

Milton

Haybrook

Crohill

The Postman

Richards

The village shop stood on this site from at least the mid-1800s. The Battell family (who still live in the village today) took it over in 1913 and ran it until 1975. In its heyday it sold petrol, paraffin, chicken, hardware, clothes and shoes. In fact, if you can name it, they probably sold it.

Fennessy

Spaul

Terry Hanner and Lenny Talbot

P. Battell

Beckham

Post office day at the chapel

G. Nobbs

33

Denton United Reformed Church

Milton

Chapelgoers

Pointer

Hill

Chapel interior with Millennium Banners

Baker

Geoffrey and Valerie Fairhead driving the cattle

A. Fairhead

The milkman

Spaul

Chapel Farm

Carden

Richard Carden with Allen scythe

Carden

Betty Syrett in The Walk

Cargill

Geoffrey Fairhead
A. Fairhead

Crohill

Anne Carden and Liz Cargill riding out of The Walk
Carden

Seamons

Austen

Scenes from Haggards Farm, formerly owned by Rider Haggard

Pockthorpe Cottage

Collins

Mencher

Mencher

Chapel Hill

Mencher

Entrance to Pockthorpe Lane

Kent

37

Jenny Crohill, Carol Collins, Sally and Adrian Haigh *Crohill*

Bridge over the Beck *Mencher*

Sarah Boyall *Boyall*

Tim and Hilda Thomas   *Crohill*

Thomas   *Milton*

Chapel Hill Farm

Haymaking   *Crohill*

Wendy Wright and Sheila Seaman   *Seaman*   Michael Pointer and Roy Day   *R. Day*

John and Kathleen Pointer, Molly Gunton, Dot Holmes,   *B. Gunton*
Reg Gunton and Brenda Day

Rosenda, Paynes Hill   *R. Day*

John Pointer at Paynes Hill Farm   *R. Day*

Manor Farm   *Fearnley*

Rosie Fearnley   *Fearnley*

Rosie Fearnley   *Fearnley*

John Fearnley   *Fearnley*

41

Rachel Fearnley creating the Parish Magazine

Meg Wright and daughter Hilary

Meg Wright

Walnut Tree Farm Barns

Boyall

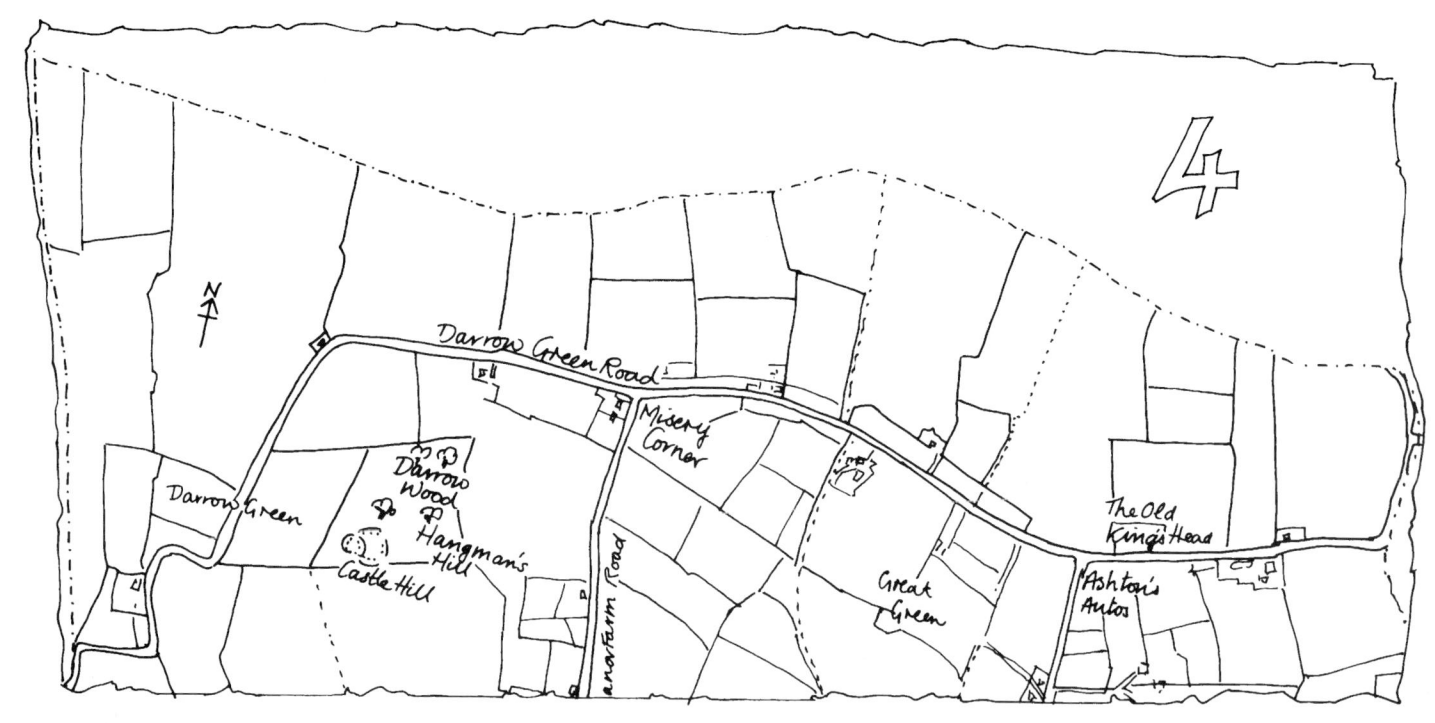

The map shows the following labels: Darrow Green Road, Misery Corner, Darrow Green, Darrow Wood, Hangman's Hill, Castle Hill, Manor Farm Road, Great Green, The Old King's Head, Ashton's Autos

Aerial view of Denton's old motte and bailey castle

Entrance to Lammas Farm   *R. Wright*

Colin Wright   *R. Wright*

THE NATIONAL TRUST

DARROW WOOD

THE NATIONAL TRUST
OPEN TO THE PUBLIC
(SUBJECT TO THE BYELAWS
ON THE BACK OF THIS NOTICE)
PLEASE AVOID
LEAVING LITTER
LIGHTING FIRES
DAMAGING TREES
OR PLANTS

Carden

Layland

Darrow Farm

David Layland

Layland

Layland

Darrow Green Farm   *Winter*

Brian Walker   *Winter*

Rear view of Darrow Mount   *Winter*

Deer Cottage and Darrow Mount   *K. Hanner*

Earl

Earl   *Earl*

The Earls at Fir Tree Farm

Pear Tree Farm   *M. Palmer*

Vera Palmer   *M. Palmer*

Brian and Peter Walker *Walker*

Alan and Matthew Squirrell and Robin Godsmark *Squirrell*

Brian Walker *Walker*

Ivy Farm *Squirrell*

Roger Dove in his workshop

Dove

The Old Dairy

Dove

Kathryn Dove

Dove

51

Dove

Les Baker at Oak Lodge

Hill

Mutts Farm

D. Parsons

The Kitchen, Mutts Farm

D. Parsons

Scarfe

Grant

Nigel Seamons watching the World Cup on TV   *Grant*

Ken Ashton photographing the happy couple   *Grant*   53

Silver Wedding Celebration for David and Margaret Parsons

Mutts Farm

P. Parsons

Charman

Karen and Kathryn Dove

Cargill

Anthony Hill and friends

Cargill

Keith Ellis and Liz Cargill at Mutts Farm *Parsons*

James Godsmark *Godsmark*

Pond, Mill Farm *Drew*

The Bungalow *Drew*

Darrow Green Road

Marijke

Day

Day

Mill House

Bill Day

Day

Terry Hanner and John Pointer   *K. Hanner*

Woodgate   *K. Hanner*

                                                  K. Hanner

57

Casa Mia   *K. Hanner*

Penlea

Woodruff

Charity, Francesca and Arabella Woodruff

Woodruff

Ronay   *Roper*

Kevin Roper   *Roper*

Charlish

Jan Ramsay and Doris Battell   *Charlish*

The Old King's Head, one of two public houses in the village and formerly a drover's inn. It closed in 1984   *Charlish*

Sylvia and Don Basinger   *Basinger*

Miss Moll who died aged 91 shortly after this picture was taken   *M. Hanner*

61

Denton and Alburgh Community Bus   *Squirrell*

Godsmark

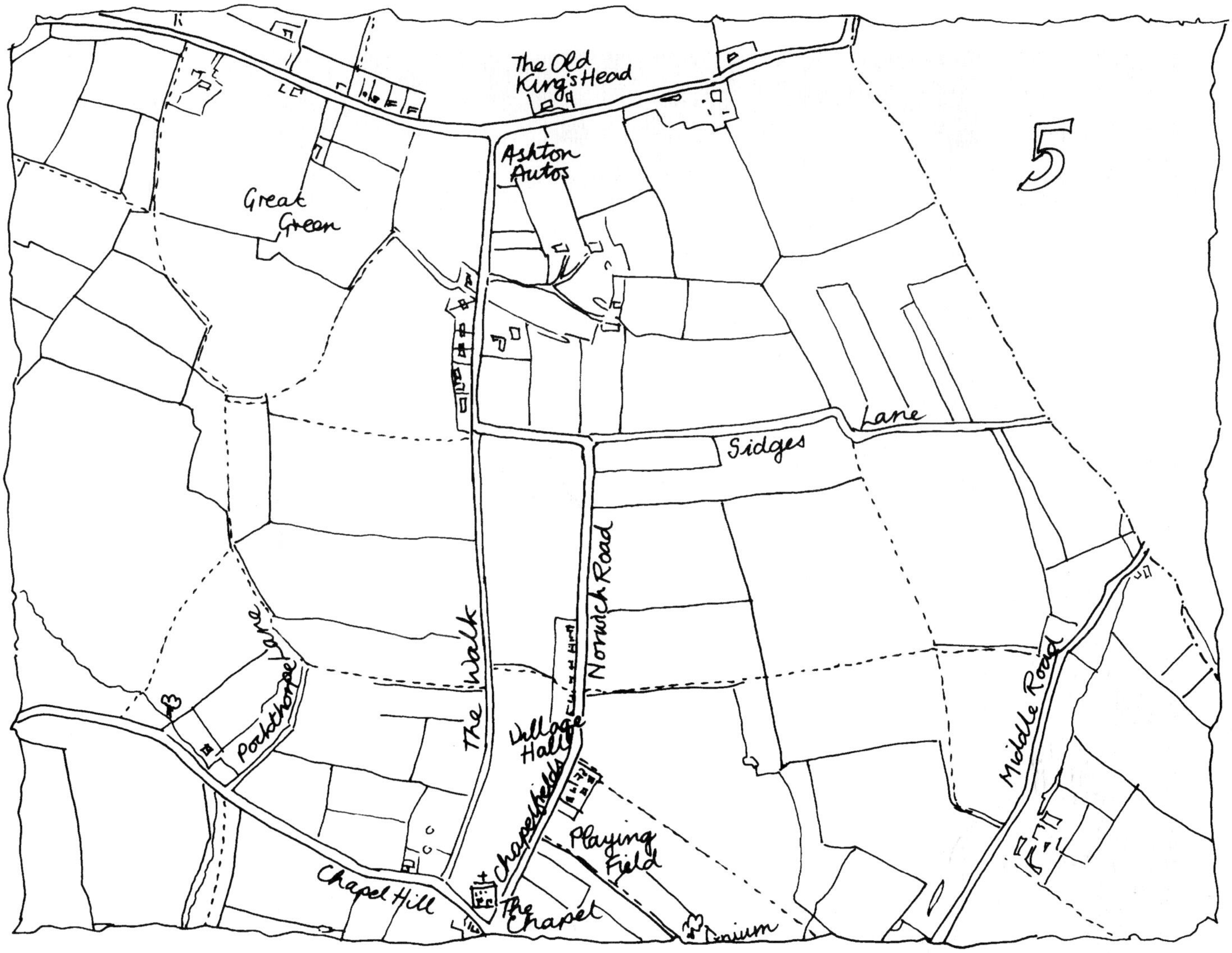

The Old King's Head

Ashton Autos

Great Green

Sidges Lane

Norwich Road

The Walk

Pockthorpe Lane

Village Hall

Middle Road

Chapel Hill

Chapelfield

The Chapel

Playing Field

Chapel Hill

Charlish

Ken Ashton *Scarfe*

Hazell's garden, Upland Terrace *Hazell*

Upland Farm *Howman*

Jonathan and Malcolm Skinner *Skinner*

Skinner Malcolm Skinner *Talbot*

Glebe Farm *Skinner*

8 Upland Terrace *Millington*

Lenny Talbot *Talbot*

Sunday bowls, 6 Upland Terrace *Talbot*

Kathy Rose, Joy Talbot, Desmond Talbot and Ronnie Sheldrake *M. Hanner*

Ivan Talbot *Talbot*

5 and 6 Upland Terrace   *Bennison*

Martin and Jennifer Bennison   *Bennison*

Willa and Beth, Jaide, Emma and Liam   *Bennison*

Liam Bennison and Edward Howman   *Howman*

Bennison

Upland Terrace, Willa King-Hall

Millington

Alan Lawrence

Whiting

Leroy and Alan Lawrence

Whiting

Upland Terrace

Whipps

Rose Cottage garden   *Bardsley*

Malcolm Bardsley   *Bardsley*

Jackie Block and Emily Downing   *Downing*

Sunbeam Cottage   *Downing*

Whitegate Corner   *Peck*

Angela, Ruth, Craig and Lisa Fennessy   *Fennessy*

Fennessy   *Fennessy*

Gary and Kate Peck, Walnut Tree Cottage

Townsend

Pauline and Terry Townsend

Townsend

Dawniwood and The Cottage

Collins

71

David Lambert and Doris Battell   *Haigh*

Adrian Haigh   *Haigh*

Stewart Downing, Adrian Haigh and Terry Hanner   *Haigh*

Doris, Anna, Peggy and Ben Battell, and Mary Alderton   *Lambert*

Anna at Greenways   *Gilbert*

Whitsands   *Welsh*

73

Peter and Christine Hipwell   *Hipwell*

Norwich Road   *Rumsby*

Tim Whiteman   *Whiteman*

Overdale   *Hipwell*

The Village Hall   *Hooker*

                                                                                                   Kent

Aerial view with marquee for Midsummer celebration   *Morgan*

John Jennings, Rita Garland

K. Hanner

Friday night football, Hipwell boys   A. Hipwell

Peter and Pat Townsend   A. Hipwell

Friday night in the bar   Martin

The Bowls Team

Charlish

K. Hanner

Reg and Bubbles Gunton's 50th Wedding Celebration

Jennings

Peggy Battell's 80th birthday lunch   *K. Hanner*

Charlie and Dulcie Rogers with Molly Gunton   *K. Hanner*

Margaret Parsons, Barbara Spaul, Ken Ashton, Julie Oxley   *K. Hanner*
and Angus McGill

Suzy Norris and David Battell with Terry Hanner   *K. Hanner*

James, Adele, Gwen and David Godsmark   *K. Hanner*

Sarah Hanner and Daniel Morgan   *K. Hanner*

Warren coal lorry

Lazaretti

View of Globe House

M. Gunton

Bubbles and Reg Gunton

B. Gunton

Lizzy Nobbs

R. Sheldrake

Phyllis Snelling

Lloyd

Peel

Lizzy and Jean Nobbs

E. Nobbs

George Nobbs with Sarah and Steven

E. Nobbs

Cecil and June Lloyd   *Lloyd*

Molly Gunton   *B. Gunton*

Lloyd

Cecil Lloyd   *Lloyd*

Fish and Chip van   *M. Pearson*

Entrance to Playing Field   *G. Nobbs*

Recycling; Gemma Broadley   *Broadley*

Denton Playing Field   *Squirrell*

Lazaretti   VJ Black Poplar   *Lazaretti*

The Old Coal Shed   *Collins*

Seaman

The hornbeam, planted in the centre of the grove

Milton

The red oak given by Denton, Texas

Ashton

The wood is planted

Carden

Denton Millennium Wood

Lazaretti

Rio Lazaretti   *Lazaretti*

17 Chapelfields   *Capenhurst*

Capenhurst

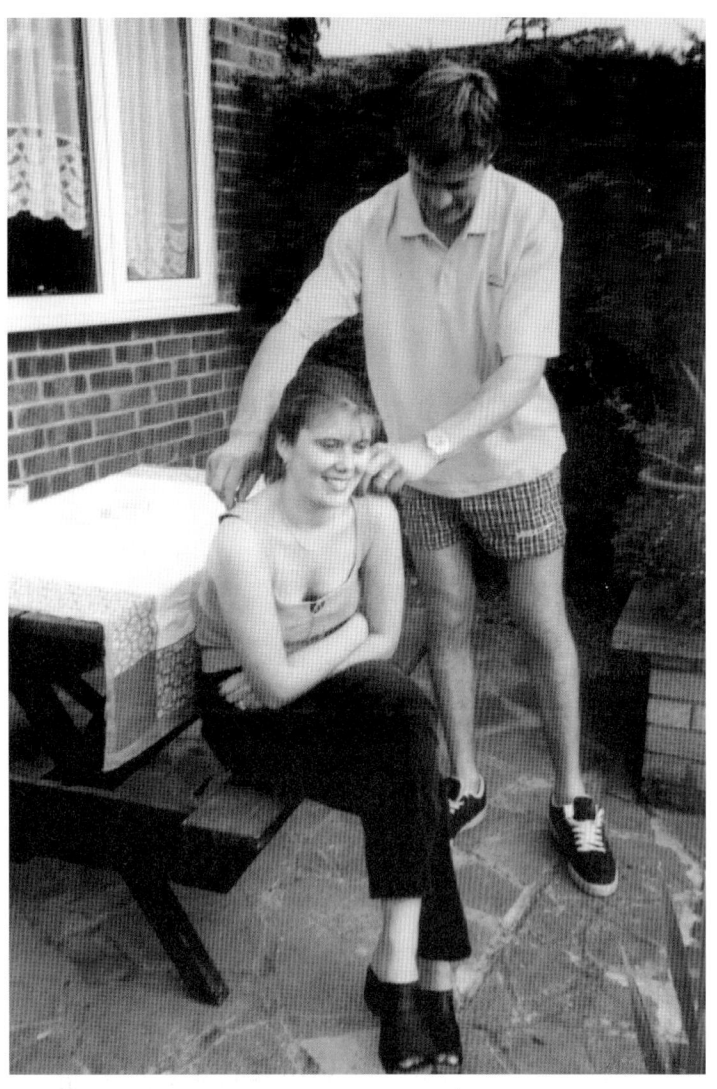

Tanya and Andrew Knights *Seaman*

The Weeping Pear *Baker*

Ron Cork *Cork*

Brian Cork *Cork*

G. Nobbs

The wedding of Tanya Seaman and Andrew Knights (with the Hill family's Classic Carriage)

Baker

11 Chapelfields

Seaman

1 and 2 Chapelfields   *Beckham*

Powell   *Powell*

3 Chapelfields   *Markwell*

Markwell

Powell

The Patch

Kent

Mobile library

Haigh

Street Farm

Baker

Syrett

John and Laura Barber

J. Barber

J. Barber

Laura and Sally Barber, David, Kirstin and Ewan Cumming

Cumming

Stephen Broadley   *Broadley*

Tri Ffordd and 2 Chapel Corner   *Syrett*

Gemma Broadley, Rio Lazaretti and Andrew Broadley   *Broadley*

Early morning traffic jam   *Cumming*

Julie Cooper, Molly Gunton, Gwen Roberts, Ivan Talbot, Vera Vass   *McGill*

The Postmistress, Julie Cooper   *P. Battell*

Meg Wright and Kathleen Pointer   *P. Battell*

Post Office at the Chapel   *Collins*

Durack

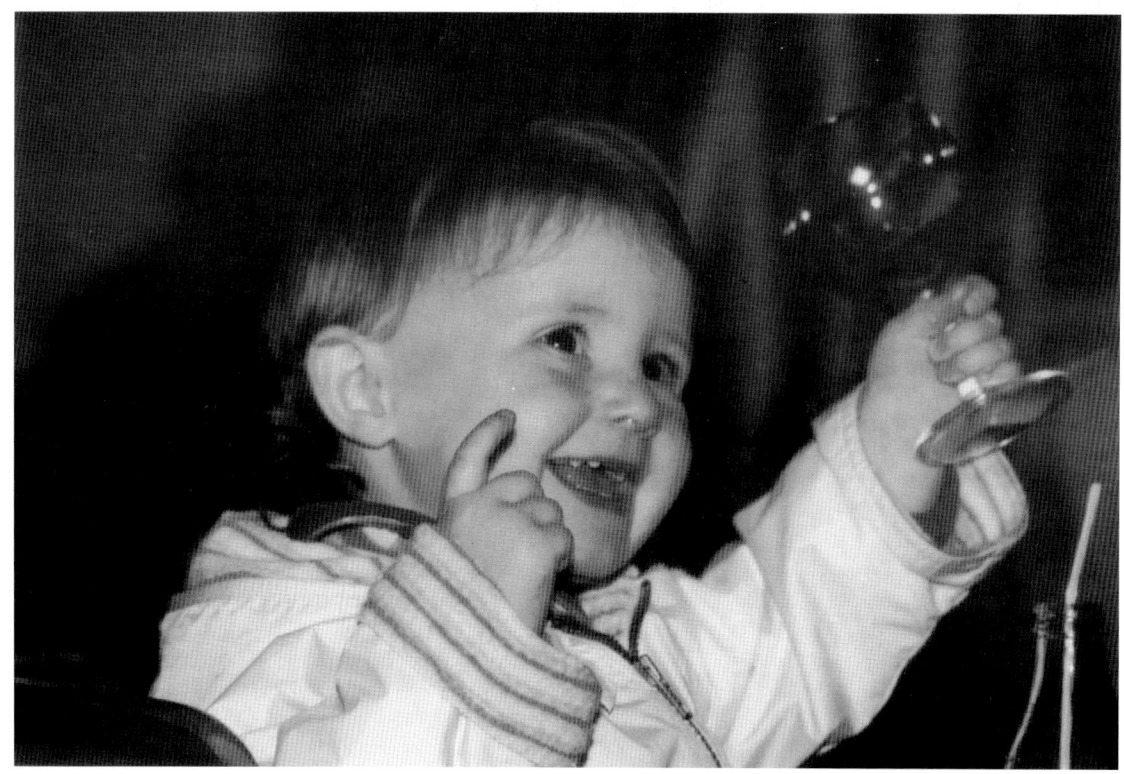

Here's to the Millennium; Nicole Stribling

Martin

Village noticeboard

Ashton

Malcolm Bardsley   *Godsmark*

THE MILLENNIUM EVE

Millennium Eve began with the traditional party at Denton Village Hall. As midnight approached villagers processed by candlelight to Whitegate Corner. At midnight we lit the Millennium Beacon and celebrated with champagne. Despite the damp night it was a wonderful way to see in the century. The party carried on in the open air until the small hours.

Adrian and Gill Hipwell   *Godsmark*

Matthew and Hazel Squirrell, Chris Bardsley and Anthony Hill *Godsmark*

Annie Whiteman, Jean Lambert, Kath Hanner and others making hot chocolate *Godsmark*

DJ Matt *Godsmark*

Denise and Peter Grant with Pauline Townsend *Godsmark*

2nd January 2000
SERVICE OF LIGHT
A fourteen foot cross covered in white chrysanthemums dominated the church for the Service of Light on the evening of 2nd January 2000. As people came in they were all given lighted candles. This service emphasised for many people the spiritual side of millennium celebrations.

Bardsley   *Bardsley*

Bardsley

Murray Gray, the Striblings, David Parsons, Trudi Borsberry and Brian Hewlett   *Jennings*

Ashton   Rue and Fleur Guyton   *Carden*

Children from Alburgh with Denton First School   *Ashton*

Planting the Millennium Wood, February 2000

Haigh

Organisers Terry and Kath Hanner

Haigh

Haigh

Haigh

Exhibition of Old Village Photos, March 2000

99

David Cumming and Steve Whiteman *Whiteman*

Gill Hipwell *Whiteman*

Mandy and Chris Woodruff, *Whiteman*
Adele Godsmark

Bill Day, David Godsmark *Whiteman*

Millennium Book Launch and Barbecue, May 2000

Thomas

EXHIBITION OF LOCAL CRAFTS
May 2000

To celebrate local talent and skills, everyone in the village was invited to contribute to an exhibition of local crafts. From model boats to musical instruments, tapestry to painting – the range of exhibits showed amazing talent from all ages. The weather did its worst but the exhibition was a great success.

At the same time the Chapel hosted a display of banners created in the village to celebrate the history of Christianity.

On the Saturday evening the Church hosted an 'Easy Listening' concert featuring a number of local talents. It was a brilliant weekend!

Hill

K. Hanner

Village Crafts Exhibition

Thomas

1. The Nativity

2. The Resurrection

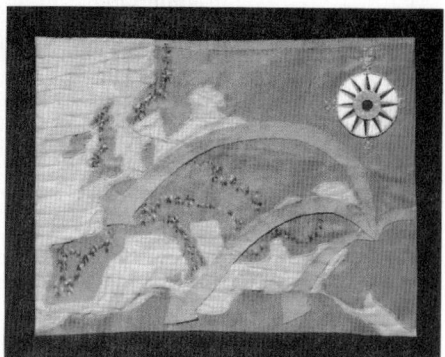

3. The Spreading of the Gospel

4. Saint Augustine 597A.D.

5. The Translation of the Bible

6. Henry VIII

7. Elizabeth I

8. John & Charles Wesley

9. Denton L.E.P. 1986

Display of Banners in the Chapel, May 2000

Rev. Ian Bentley *Dove*

Sarah Whiteman *Dove*

The Choir *Dove*

Eddie Winter *Dove*

Stephen Easton *Dove*

Easy Listening Concert, May 2000

Lambert

Spaul

Godsmark

Betty Wilby and Doris Battell

Whiteman

Lambert

Preparations for Midsummer Celebration

Barbara and Jeremy Charlish   *Jennings*

Janet, Richard and Edward   *K. Hanner*
Howman

Lucy and Sarah Hanner,   *K. Hanner*
Robin Godsmark

James Hanner, Lenny Talbot   *K. Hanner*

Michael, Lindsey and Jean Hanner   *K. Hanner*

Lisa and Ruth Fennessy   *K. Hanner*

Ben Battell with Fran Tracy   *K. Hanner*

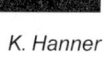

Clare, Malcolm and Janet Skinner   *K. Hanner*

Peggy and Ben Battell   *K. Hanner*

John and Val Carslake *Ashton*   Fiona Easton, Mandy Smith *Jennings*

Emily and Simon Winter, Malcolm Skinner, Jayne Rayner *Jennings*   Phil Morgan, Rita Garland *Jennings*

Steve, Siobhan, Davina and Katrina Cattermole *Jennings*

Derek and Margaret Hazell *Ashton*

Rachel Cable, Mick Loades *Ashton*

Doreen and Tony Last, Michael Hanner and family, *K. Hanner*
Geoffrey and Valerie Fairhead

Greta and Peter Parsons *Ashton*

Peter and Pat Townsend, Dot Sheldrake, Glenys Sheldrake, *K. Hanner*
Lindsey Hanner and Ernie Sheldrake

June Lloyd, Molly Gunton, Daisy Parkins, Diane Charman, *Ashton*
Norma Capenhurst and Phyllis Snelling

Angela Fennessy and Betty Wilby   *K. Hanner*

Daisy Parkins, Diane Charman and Norma Capenhurst   *K. Hanner*

Richard Parsons, Helen Lambert, Lisa Fennessy,   *K. Hanner*
Christopher Ashton

                    K. Hanner

Maureen Seamons, Pearl Charnick, Shirley Boyall   *K. Hanner*

Kevin Hanner, Jane Dennison   *K. Hanner*

Vera and Mike Palmer, Shirley and Andrew Palmer   *K. Hanner*

Tim and Hilda Thomas, Les and Brenda Baker,   *K. Hanner*
Marlene Balls, Brian Hewlett, John Pointer, Malcolm Balls

Matthew, Heather and Alan Squirrell   *K. Hanner*

Shirley and Bob Boyall, Tony Charnick and Nigel Seamons   *K. Hanner*

Lucy and Michael Hanner   *K. Hanner*

Lenny Talbot and Jennifer Bennison   *K. Hanner*

110

Preparing for the toast – Anne Carden *Ashton*

The toast – Stephen Easton *Ashton*

Jan Ramsey, Sid Scarfe *Ashton*

The auction. Richard Carden and Matthew Smith *Ashton*

James and Jonathan Hanner, Matthew Smith, Ben Battell, Ian Cooper, Robin Godsmark, Kevin Hanner

K. Hanner

Phil Morgan, Mandy Smith, Barbara Spaul and David Godsmark

Ashton

MILLENNIUM FETE AND SPORTS

As usual the Denton Fête was held on the village playing field on 8th July. To add to the fun, the fête included a special millennium sports. Despite the damp weather at the start it was a fun day and raised funds for the Church, Chapel and Village Hall.

Matthew Smith *Spaul*

Doris Battell, Denise Grant *Jennings*

K. Hanner

113

Jennings

The Stribling girls, Harry Ramsay, Matthew Dove, Kris Hanner, Melissa Hanner

D. Parsons

K. Hanner

Jennings

Whipps

Reg Gunton, Jane Dennison, James Hanner   *K. Hanner*

Sarah and Lucy Hanner   *K. Hanner*

The Plant Stall   *Spaul*

Rita Garland, Jean Whipps, Louis de Bernières-Smart   *Parsons*

Robin Godsmark,   *K. Hanner*
Kevin Hanner

115

Robert Aldous and Robert Sherwood

Bardsley

James Godsmark, Adrian Hipwell, Chris Whipps, Gill Hipwell

Godsmark

Bardsley

Bardsley

116

Bardsley

Before the start of the walk

Bardsley

The last ones to finish!

Godsmark

Last day for Sam's old bus   *Godsmark*

DENTON SERVICES

These are some of the services the villagers of Denton rely on. Other services are reflected elsewhere in the book.

What's missing?
    Gerry the Fishman.
    Derek Whyte – Sunday papers, who has served the village for over 50
        years.
    The Hemglas Frozen Food Van.

The refuse collection   *Carslake*

Collecting the recycling   *Carslake*

Postal delivery   *M. Palmer*

Nick Frere-Smith, blacksmith   *Thomas*

The milkman, Turrell's Dairy   *D. Battell*   Terry Hanner, the paperboy   *Whiteman*

List of Contributing Households

Ashton	Gibson	Peel
Austen	Gilbert	Pointer, G
Baker	Godsmark	Pointer, K
Balls	Grant	Powell
Barber, J	Gregory	Reeder
Barber, T	Gunton, M	Ready
Bardsley	Gunton, B	Richards
Basinger	Guyton	Roper
Battell, D	Haigh	Rumsby
Battell, P	Hanner, M	Scarfe
Beckham	Hanner, K	Seaman
Borsberry	Hazell	Seamons
Boyall	Hewlett	Shaw
Broadley	Hicks	Sheldrake, E
Bruty	Hill	Sheldrake, R
Cable	Hipwell, A	Skinner
Capenhurst	Hipwell, P	Smeeth
Carden	Hooker	Snelling
Cargill	Howman	Spaul
Carslake	Jefferson	Sprake
Cattermole	Jennings	Squirrell
Charlish	Jones	Staley, Philip
Charman	Kent	Stribling
Charnick	Knights	Sutton
Clues	Lambert	Syrett
Cole	Layland	Talbot, D., I. & L
Collins	Lazaretti	Thomas
Cork	Lloyd	Townsend
Crohill	Markwell	Valori
Cumming	Martin	Walker
Darell	Mayhew	Wallace
Day, R	McGill	Weigman
Day, W	Mencher	Welsh
De Bernières-Smart	Milton	Whipps
Dove	Morgan	Whiteman
Downing	Nobbs, E	Whiting
Drew	Nobbs, G	Wilby
Durack	Palmer, A	Winter
Easton	Palmer, M	Woodruff
Fairhead, A	Parsons, D	Wright, M
Fairhead, G	Parsons, P	Wright, C
Fearnley	Pearson	Wright, J
Fennessy	Peck	